PROJECT DELIVERY, UNCERTAINTY AND NEUROSCIENCE

PROJECT DELIVERY, UNCERTAINTY AND NEUROSCIENCE

A Leader's Guide to Walking in Fog

Carole Osterweil

VISIBLE DYNAMICS

Publisher's note

Visible Dynamics
2 Liscombe West
Liscombe Park
Leighton Buzzard

LU7 0JL, United Kingdom

This edition first published in 2019 by Visible Dynamics

www.visibledynamics.co.uk

Cover design and typesetting: Nick Mortimer

ISBN 978-1-9160210-1-3

Praise for *Project Delivery, Uncertainty And Neuroscience*

"Neuroscience provides a fascinating way of thinking about projects, and this book offers great insight into key aspects of performance. The 'softer' side of project management is vital, yet clear thinking and advice on the subject is rare. Uncertainty is a fact of life in projects and embracing this truth (and its consequences) is essential. There are many great nuggets to take away here, along with very practical tools for leaders to improve their project outcomes."

DR NEIL TURNER, CRANFIELD UNIVERSITY

"Carole Osterweil's highly original book helps you get inside the mind of the project. If you understand your own and everyone else's hang ups (biases, attitudes to risk, perceptions of value) then you can start to influence how people behave within the project."

JONATHAN NORMAN, MAJOR PROJECTS KNOWLEDGE HUB

"We talk about a VUCA world, and how major government and organisational projects are started with the best of intents but get bogged down. Project Delivery, Uncertainty and Neuroscience highlights recent neurological research and gives insight into how to use it in project delivery. Read it and learn how to balance attention to the technical with attention to the behavioural and social."

SARAH COLEMAN, BUSINESS EVOLUTION

"In Project Delivery, Uncertainty and Neuroscience Carole Osterweil has managed to demystify the emergent property of Project Braininess. You need to read this book."

PROFESSOR EDDIE OBENG, PENTACLE, VIRTUAL BUSINESS SCHOOL

This book is easy to read and full of practical, relevant insights. I like the illustrations of key points using recent research. For me, the most useful part of the book was the spectrum from certainty to uncertainty, and how to create certainty when so little is definite..This is book is a helpful contribution to understanding how to lead complex projects. I recommend it to project and programme managers, risk managers and change professionals.

MELANIE FRANKLIN, AGILE CHANGE MANAGEMENT LTD

"I am constantly amazed at how much time, effort and money is thrown at structural issues (time, pace, scope etc) and how little at the messy socio-political where the vast majority of problems occur. It's great to find a well written book that gets to grips with this."

STEPHEN CARVER, CRANFIELD UNIVERSITY

Contents

List of Illustrations

Introduction

We're often told that success in delivering complex projects, change and transformation programmes, depends on the quality of leadership. Research by the Management Innovation Centre in Amsterdam gives precise insight into the skills that make the difference[1]. It examined 2,000 projects in 43 countries before concluding that the best opportunity for improving success rates lies in learning to understand and influence social dynamics (why people behave as they do).

These findings are supported by research into early warning signs for complex projects[2], which concluded that:

- formal review processes will be ineffective until we learn to pick up on subtle dynamics such as groupthink, political pressure and inconsistent decision-making alongside progress, risk and finance
- too many of us are blind to these human and organisational dynamics
- the main challenge to improving performance is in our heads

These conclusions present all leaders endeavouring to deliver complex projects and programmes with a challenge. If we cannot see these dynamics playing out, how do we know they are real, and how can we influence them?

Ten years ago, you could be forgiven for dismissing talk of such dynamics in organisations as 'fluffy'. Times have changed.

Advances in neuroscience mean we are increasing our understanding of how the human brain works and we are seeing evidence that these dynamics exist. In addition, the trend is for organisations to embark on increasingly risky and uncertain ventures. These include many utilising digital technologies and many pushing the boundaries of engineering.

These two factors have profound implications for all leaders including programme and project professionals. Successful delivery requires leaders who understand how social dynamics arise and leaders who are skilled at influencing them. Yet to date, few have been schooled in these disciplines.

This guide aims to demystify the whole arena.

Its origins go back to Project 2020, which I worked on several years ago

Project 2020 was a run by a senior team. Its remit was to restructure a partnership organisation delivering health and social care across the NHS, central, regional and local government.

Government policy was changing so fast that every time the team got a clear sense of the way forward, there'd be a new policy announcement and the goalposts shifted. For the team, who'd been schooled in traditional project management methods it was a nightmare.

How could they deliver?

They were desperate for clear parameters, but the Steering Group were unable to oblige. The environment was moving too fast and, no matter how much they wished otherwise, there was little they could do to influence it.

Many of my clients over the last ten years have faced challenges like those of the Project 2020 team. They are talented, experienced and highly-motivated teams and individuals, charged with delivering ambitious objectives in relentless and demanding environments.

They work in 'messy' environments which frequently don't conform to expectations about how business environments are supposed to function. Some operate in formal project structures, others do not. Either way, the disconnect between how their organisation or project is supposed to function and what happens in practice can often leave them feeling stuck, frustrated and unable to put a finger on what is going wrong or why. It's as if a thick fog has descended yet they must keep walking - despite being unable to see a way forward.

If you recognise aspects of yourself in this description, this guide is for you.

It is a resource in three parts.

Part One is a primer. It provides a high-level introduction to how the human brain works and uses this as a platform to explore the dynamics of complexity, and attitudes to risk and uncertainty. Three factors which have a fundamental impact on stress levels and project outcomes.

Part Two is primarily a toolkit. It includes a series of frameworks and suggestions to help you apply your knowledge about how the brain works. Its aim is to develop your capability to read and influence social dynamics, so you can reduce complexity and improve outcomes.

Part Three is a summary of key lessons from parts one and two.

Part One – Primer

Brain Basics

The starting point for making sense of social dynamics is a high-level understanding of how the human brain works.

I find it particularly helpful to visualise the brain as having three key parts[3], each with a distinct function as shown in *Figure 1*.

- The *primitive* brain ensures body processes such as breathing and heart function are maintained
- The *feeling* brain acts as our emotional command centre and is where impulsive actions begin
- The *thinking* brain where higher functions such as analysis, creativity, logical decision-making and empathy originate

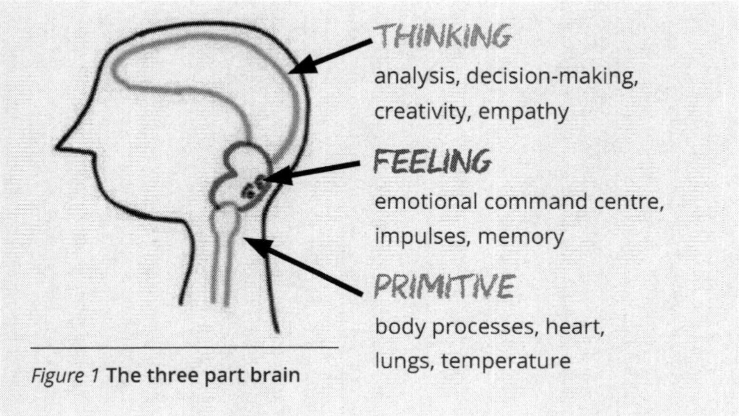

Figure 1 **The three part brain**

The three parts are intimately connected and linked to the body. Together they operate as an integrated system. Acting in consort their primary concern is to ensure our survival through a structure which can be traced back to our hunter-gatherer ancestors.

We're familiar with the human fight/flight/freeze response and we know it is driven by the need for physical survival.

We're learning from recent advances in neuroscience that the human brain does not distinguish between physical and psychological survival. It uses the same wiring to deal with physical and social threats.

The amygdala which sits in the *feeling* brain is constantly scanning the environment to identify things, people and situations to avoid and those it is safe to approach. It operates on autopilot and outside of conscious awareness. It continually assesses threat levels and makes judgements about what is safe and what is not. As soon as our amygdala assesses a threat level as too high, it kicks our survival response into action.

Our body processes change. Our heart rate increases and our breathing gets shallower. Energy is diverted away from our *thinking* brain. Our field of vision narrows, we become distracted and we are less able to think clearly as without realizing it, we become preoccupied with survival. At the same time the amygdala triggers avoidance emotions such as fear, anger, or shame and these are accompanied by changes in our behavior.

We unwittingly adopt avoidance behaviours – we might become defensive, or if our amygdala judges the threat to be strong enough, we might go on to the attack or withdraw from the situation completely.

Crucially the brain's definition of a threat is determined by prior experience and is very individual. Working at speed the amygdala doesn't stop to test whether a threat is real.

For example, seeing a client flinch momentarily as you present performance figures might spark a defensive reaction in you, but have no impact on a colleague at the same meeting. There's no saying what impact you barking a response to your client's questions will have. They might take it their stride, they might not.

However, not all situations provoke avoidance behaviours. When the amygdala assesses the situation as familiar and safe the opposite happens. Our reflex is to approach and seek reward. The associated emotions are trust, love, excitement and joy. Emotions we tend to associate with the relationship between a mother/father and baby rather than adults in the corporate world.

When these emotions are coursing through the body we are highly motivated and at ease, our *thinking* brain can operate at its best. We are creative, collaborative and able to learn together.

Dan Siegel's terminology is helpful to contrast these two states[4]. When responding to threats we 'flip our lid', the *thinking* brain is taken 'offline' and productivity drops. When the sense of threat recedes and the flow of energy to our *thinking* brain is restored the *thinking* brain comes back 'online' as shown in *Figure 2*.

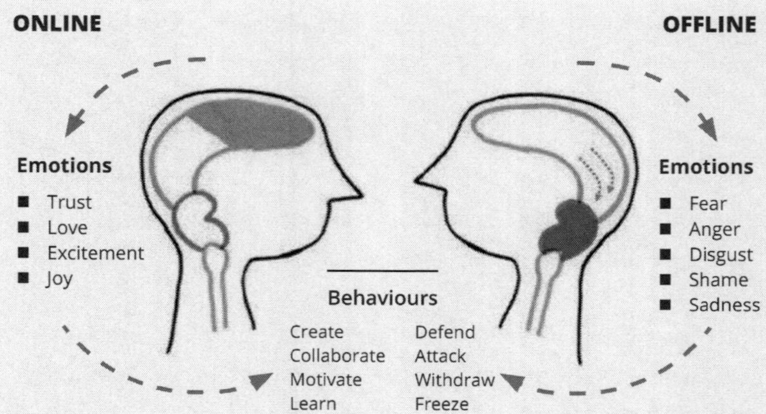

Figure 2 **Emotions and behaviours change when the *thinking* brain goes offline**
Source: Visible Dynamics

The brain uses the same wiring to deal with physical and social threats. In the 21st Century workplace we recognise and legislate for physical threats, just think of Health and Safety for example. Yet the notion of social threat is new to most of us – despite its impact on behavior and productivity.

What constitutes social threat?

David Rock casts light on the sources of social threat. He highlights five factors that the brain is always monitoring[5] that have a huge impact on how we behave. He summarises them with the mnemonic SCARF.

We are acutely sensitised to

> **Status** – the perception of being considered better or worse than others

Certainty – the predictability of future events
Autonomy – the level of control we feel able to exert over our lives
Relatedness – the sense of being able to share goals and being connected with others
Fairness – the sense that we are being respected and treated fairly in comparison to others

When people sense a change in any one of the SCARF factors, it can activate an avoidance response – The bigger the change the stronger the response!

Picture Stefan who has arrived on time for a performance review meeting. His new manager has been in post six weeks, yet they've spent hardly any time together. Looking through the door Stefan sees someone else is in the room and is in the middle of a very animated conversation. The longer Stefan waits the more unsettled he becomes.

His manager's unthinking actions have challenged his sense of status (S). As time goes on Stefan becomes less certain (C) about what to expect and how the meeting is likely to pan out. He feels less in control of his destiny (A).

When the meeting eventually starts, Stefan's *thinking* brain is not fully online. He finds it harder to gather his thoughts, hear positive feedback or think collaboratively. His manager finds him defensive.

We see and respond to social threat in the most mundane situations. These threats do not have to be explicit, intentional or real. We only have to perceive that our status has been reduced or that we are being treated unfairly and we will respond with avoidance behaviours.

The converse is also true. When we believe we are being treated fairly and that we have a degree of control over the future it's easier to keep our *thinking* brains online. We want the feelings of excitement and trust that come with engagement.

Understanding how the brain works adds new perspectives to many good leadership practices. Take the adage 'When dealing with change communicate, communicate, communicate!'

SCARF guides us to five areas that need to inform all our actions in organisational and project settings.

For example, by highlighting our desire for certainty, SCARF tells us that the prospect of change – whether a tweak to the IT system or wholesale digital transformation is likely to activate a threat response. We need to include this knowledge in our project planning, and make sure that we prioritise activities to reduce the degree of uncertainty and counter the threat response.

This means speaking to people about the vision for the future, and sharing plans for achieving objectives; it means explicitly discussing what you do know about the future and being willing to admit what you have yet to work out; and it means offering timescales or admitting 'we can't tell you now but we will tell you by ...'

Figure 3 gives further examples for using SCARF in organisational and project settings.

	ACTIVATES THREAT	ACTIVATES REWARD
STATUS Importance relative to others	• Asking ' Do you need advice?' • Annual Performance Review • Sense of being 'left out'	• Noticing work done & improvements • Public acknowledgement • Allowing people to provide feedback on their own work
CERTAINTY Ability to predict the future	• Prospect of change • Not knowing people's expectation	• Vision, maps, plans & strategy • Making the implicit explicit • 'Can't tell you now but will tell you by ....'
AUTONOMY Exerting control over events	• Sense that stress is inescapable • Pressure to conform to team norms	• Having a choice 'which do you prefer?' • Individual 'point of need' decision-making
RELATEDNESS Sense of connection with others	• Meeting someone unknown • Feeling let down or excluded	• Shaking hands, swapping names, discussing something in common • Showing genuine interest (listening mentoring, coaching)
FAIRNESS Fair exchanges between people	• Sense of discrimination	• Increase transparency in communication • Enable groups to create their own rules • Help people see situation from other perspectives

Figure 3 SCARF in action

Source: Cecil[6]

We've seen from this introduction to neuroscience that every interaction with another person triggers a change in the intensity and quality of our emotions. Most of us are unaware of the ebbs and flows of our emotions. Yet it's these changes, driven by our innate need to survive, that determine how we behave.

At its simplest, social complexity arises from interactions between two people. However, on projects we rarely work in isolation and this introduces another layer of complexity because group and team environments amplify emotions.

Group and team environments amplify emotions

There are as many sources of social interaction and emotional triggers as people in the proverbial room (which in the modern workplace includes those we connect with digitally via email, video and social media). Emotions and behaviours are unconsciously mirrored and acted upon by others. As a result, one or two anxious or frustrated individuals can have a disproportionate impact on outcomes.

The Project Stress Cycle (illustrated in *Figure 4*) shows how this can happen through the story of Fred. As you read it, bear in mind that stress is not a bad thing per se.

Arousal, Complexity and Productivity

We've known since the early 1900's that there is a relationship between the brain's level of arousal and our ability to perform a task.

The Yerkes-Dodson law of performance shows an inverted U curve. When we have lots of time and little to do, we can find it hard to focus and performance suffers. The brain needs a degree of stimulation to operate at its best.

Too much arousal makes us stressed, anxious and even overwhelmed. It takes our *thinking* brain offline. We lose the ability to focus, we have less emotional control and we are easily triggered into avoidance behaviours. However, there is a middle ground towards the top of the inverted U where, with 'just the right amount of arousal', our *thinking* Brain stays online. We are focussed, creative and motivated by a cascade of reward emotions.

The Project Stress Cycle

Picture Fred, a senior member of the project team. Things are not going his way. He's getting increasingly frazzled. He is holding it together but doesn't realise how stressed he is. He is snapping at everyone and he's finding it harder to act in a rational manner.

The impact on those around him is palpable. No one wants to provoke an outburst, so they give him a wide berth. And of course, after a bruising meeting it's hard to keep your own *thinking* brain online. Trust is falling across the piece and relationships and communication are suffering.

When the project started Fred and his colleagues went out of their way to highlight the need to invest time in building relationships and ensuring people worked well together. They repeatedly reminded the team 'successful delivery relies on collaboration and creativity'.

But now the pressure is on and metrics are the primary focus. As relationships get strained collaboration is more difficult. Rather than waste time struggling to work together people are falling back into old habits and old silos. They are relying on approaches that worked in the past. But without quality collaboration it's hard to be truly creative.

And the word on the street? The project is unlikely to achieve the desired outcomes – which does nothing for stress levels.

Powerful stakeholders are getting nervous. They are demanding more and more information in slightly different formats to reassure themselves that things are under control. These demands distract the team from the work they should be doing and add to the stress.

They have less time and less inclination to work collaboratively and the preoccupation with spreadsheets and metrics is forcing them to adopt behaviours that reduce the chance of success and multiply stress – right across the system.

The key message is that **we need to be alert to excess stress because it can trigger a cycle that plays out across the wider project system and impacts delivery**.

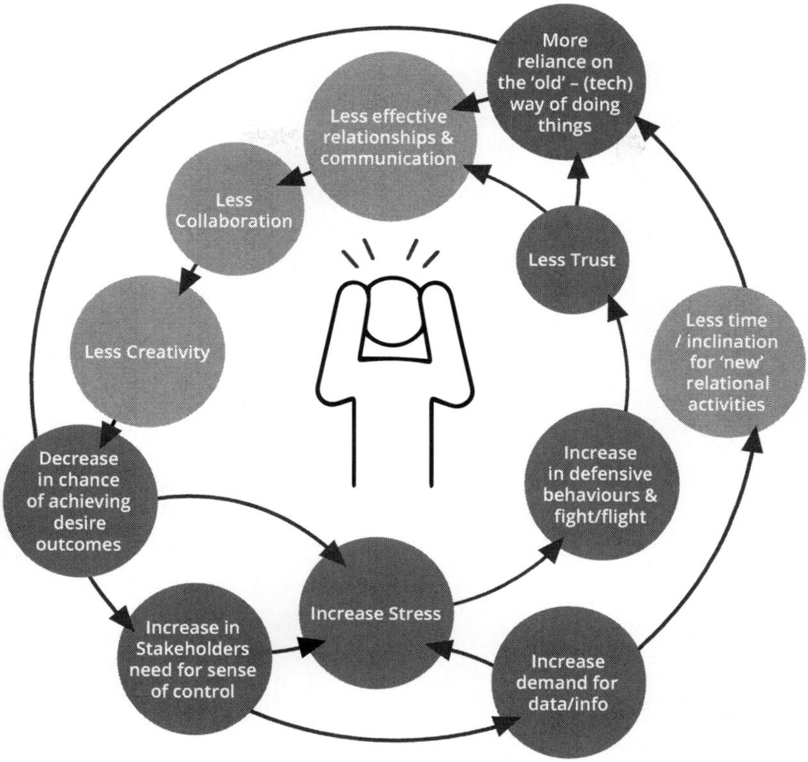

Figure 4 **The Project Stress Cycle**
Source Visible Dynamics

Some projects slide into stress cycles at crunch points (gateway reviews for example). Others can be in a chronic state of stress for years – chewing up and spitting out those charged with delivery.

Neither is surprising when seen through the lens of neuroscience. Especially when we consider the powerful stakeholders involved, the scale of investment, and the private and organisational reputations at stake.

Our innate need to belong increases complexity

In telling this story I have illustrated how the behaviour of one person can increase the complexity of delivery. Yet even this is a simplification of what happens in real life. In real life as soon as we get into team and group environments a second source of social complexity comes to the fore - our innate need to belong.

When we are in team and group environments we become sensitive to any indication, real or imagined, that we will be ostracized or ejected. (Remember the S for status and R for relatedness in SCARF).

This fear, albeit unconscious, has an impact on the dynamics. It makes us more inclined to go along with irrational decisions and dysfunctional behaviour. Often called groupthink it preserves a crucial sense of belonging - even if doing so works against the best interests of project delivery.

Viewed throught the lens of neuroscience groupthink makes perfect sense.

Where's the evidence to link neuroscience to productivity?

Take a look at Google's Project Aristotle. Project Aristotle set out to identify what makes Google's most effective project teams so effective.

Julie Rozovsky, one of the lead researchers explains the findings[7]

'After examining 180 project teams and 250 variables we discovered that who is on the team matters far less than how the team members interact, structure their work and view their contributions

It comes down to the group's norms of behaviour and five key dimensions'

> **Psychological Safety** – is it safe to take risks and be vulnerable in front of each other?
> **Dependability** – can we count on each other to do high quality work on time?
> **Structure and Clarity** – are our goals, roles and execution plans clear?
> **Meaning of the work** – are we working on something that is personally important?
> **Impact of work** – do we fundamentally believe that the work we are doing matters?

Project Aristotle demonstrated that of these five dimensions, psychological safety stands head and shoulders above the rest – it is a pre-requisite for the other four.

Part Two – Toolkit

Using Brain Knowledge to Improve Delivery

The starting point is learning to recognise when your *thinking* brain is going offline and to develop the skill to bring it back online. The skill of being 'mindful'.

With your *thinking* brain online, you will be able take an informed view of the dynamics that are playing out around you. You'll be able to

- recognise when others' *thinking* brains are offline
- make informed choices about the behaviours and interventions required to bring them back online
- see systemic patterns like the Project Stress Cycle, and
- work out how to interrupt them

Bringing Your Thinking Brain Online

Professor Mark Williams of Oxford University explains when you are mindful[8] you have 'a direct, intuitive knowing of what you are doing while you are doing it. You know what's going on inside your mind and body, and what's going on in the outside world as well.

Most of the time our attention is not where we intend it to be. Our attention is hijacked by our thoughts and emotions, by our concerns, by our worries for the future, and our regrets and memories of the past. Developing mindful awareness is about learning to pay attention, in the present moment, and without judgement. It's like training a muscle – training attention to be where you want it to be. This reduces our tendency to work on autopilot, allowing us to us choose how we respond and react.'

Techniques to bring your Thinking brain online

1. Notice the physical signs of your *thinking* brain going offline. For example, do you get a sense that your chest is tightening, or your pulse quickening? Perhaps it's a feeling that colour is rising in your cheeks, your stomach is knotting, or your jaw or fists are clenching.

2. Register 'this is important information'

3. Take a view about what to do next. You might for example:

    - Move to a different location physically and mentally. If you are sitting down, you could stand up and walk to the printer or water cooler. In a tense meeting? Suggest a five-minute comfort break. In an interview or on the phone? Shake out your wrist under the table. Or
    - Focus on your breath. Inhale, breathe deeply and exhale slowly. Do this a couple of times and then let your breathing settle into its natural rhythm. Give yourself a few moments and notice how your breath enters and leaves your body. Let your attention settle at your nostrils or your chest – it doesn't matter where. What matters is the act of noticing!

Figure 5 **Techniques to bring your *thinking* brain online**

There are numerous techniques and resources to help build your mindful awareness muscle. The steps in *Figure 5* will help you in many situations. Websites such as mindfulnet.org are a good place to start exploring this further.

Next time your project runs into difficulty, a stakeholder unexpectedly changes their position, or you are disappointed by the conclusions of a review board, STOP!

Take a minute to use your knowledge about how the brain works to consider what could be driving the situtation and what patterns might be playing out across the system.

Bringing Other People's Thinking Brains Online

With your *thinking* brain online, you are aware of your own thoughts, feeling and physical sensations and you are better equipped to read and make sense of the dynamics in the world around you.

To illustrate how this can happen let's return to the story of Project 2020. You'll recall we left it with the team desperate to deliver and caught in fog.

The Project 2020 team first glimpsed light at the end of the tunnel when, during a team meeting, I offered a label courtesy of complexity theorists Kurtz and Snowden[9] to describe their environment. It was **un-ordered**.

'In **Un-ordered environments** so much is changing on so many fronts that it seems impossible to keep up, let alone influence the way forward...

The way to thrive is to recognise that the lack of order is NOT a matter of poor investigation, inadequate resources or lack of understanding. It is simply a characteristic of a complex system at work. What's more the lack of order is not necessarily a bad thing or a problem that can be resolved if someone else would only set their mind to it.'

For the 2020 team this one word, un-ordered, was worth its weight in gold. It validated what, at some level, they had individually come to understand – the lack of order was here to stay, for the foreseeable future at least.

In one way nothing had changed – they still had to deliver.

In another, everything had shifted.

They had permission to acknowledge reality and revise their baseline assumptions. Their usual approach, which aimed to create certainty across the board would never pay off, and there was no point in pretending it would.

This recognition opened the way for a very different approach which ultimately led to a successful outcome.

My intervention with the Project 2020 team worked on several levels. It introduced a new frame of reference – that of complex systems to help make sense of the situation they found themselves in. This radically changed the way team members thought about the SCARF domain of certainty.

It created a climate where they could admit that things felt chaotic without fear of being the only person who thought the project was going off the rails. They saw that the sense of chaos reflected the state of the system, it was not caused by their inability to lead or control. They felt psychologically safe enough to speak about how stressful and difficult things were, without fear of being blamed, punished or rejected for speaking up. With *thinking* brains online, they could

- relax and stop trying to force-fit their project in its entirety to standard tools and methods
- separate the aspects of the project which were un-ordered from those which were ordered
- use standard methods where there was order
- use dialogue and sense-making elsewhere
- be confident that order would emerge

This approach has much in common with the one outlined by Mark Phillips[10] in Defining Complexity for Practitioners. Phillips explores the differences between complexity and risk. He suggests we have choices about how to treat uncertainty.

Dealing with Uncertainty

Phillips states that we can choose an orientation towards certainty or an orientation towards uncertainty. The differences are summarised in *Figure 6*. When I started working with the Project 2020 team, they fundamentally believed that all drivers of uncertainty could be identified. They were struggling to make their project fit a model that required an orientation to certainty.

They didn't realise they were doing this, and they didn't realise there was an alternative approach – why would they?

Reflecting on this and my experience of working with others facing similar challenges the metaphor of the tail wagging the dog springs to mind.

IF YOUR ORIENTATION IS TOWARDS CERTAINTY	
You fundamentally believe	• All drivers of uncertainty can be identified. • We can estimate their potential impact on outcomes and put plans place to deal with this. • There may be unknowns and unknown unknowns, but these too can be identified and managed away.
IF YOUR ORIENTATION IS TOWARDS UNCERTAINTY	
You fundamentally believe	• The drivers of uncertainty cannot be identified ahead of time. • It's not possible or desirable to plan how best to deal with an unforeseen event before it occurs. Doing so will constrain you in delivering ambitious results.

Figure 6 **An orientation towards certainty or uncertainty**

Source: Visible Dynamics

There is a place for traditional risk management, but too often it's the default approach. When setting up and delivering ambitious and complex projects it's crucial that the key players are comfortable with some things being unknowable. They need an orientation towards uncertainty.

This allows a clear definition of the 'dog' through candid discussion about the unknowns and the flexibility to deal with whatever might arise. With this framework in place, traditional risk management with its ability to identify and deal with knowable risks comes into its own.

When we work on complex projects without this over-arching framework, traditional risk management can push stakeholders into conflict as new and unforeseen challenges appear, especially if they lack the trust and ability to explore perceived risks in depth.

To avoid the risk management tail wagging the dog, we must build environments which are oriented towards uncertainty at the outset.

Building Environments Oriented Towards Uncertainty

I find it particularly helpful to use a framework that combines Eddie Obeng's project typology[11] with Ralph Stacey's work on complexity[12] to

- consider the nature of the project at hand – in terms of complexity
- people's individual preferences

Stacey suggests the two dimensions for considering the nature of complexity shown in *Figure 7*.

- the degree of divergence of view (about the way forward, processes to be used etc)
- the degree of uncertainty about the future

Both are subjective. I focus primarily on the second.

People working on the same project often have very different views about where to position the project on these two axes – especially when they come from different organisations, different stakeholder groups or even different levels or specialities within the same organisation.

We know from the discussion in Part One that perceived social threats, from any of the SCARF domains, has the potential to evoke avoidance emotions and behaviours (remember Fred and the Project Stress Cycle). Unconscious assumptions about certainty inevitably guide every aspect of our work.

Learning to surface and explore assumptions about certainty are crucial skills for project professionals. Doing so helps to create the psychological safety to enable all involved in project delivery to contextualise and better understand the challenges.

Exploring the Project at Hand

I encourage exploration of two positions on *Figure 7*. The top right where there is pressure to deliver even though we are peering into a future we cannot predict (like the Project 2020 team), and the bottom left where we have absolute clarity and clear agreement about the way forward (the terrain of traditional project management processes)

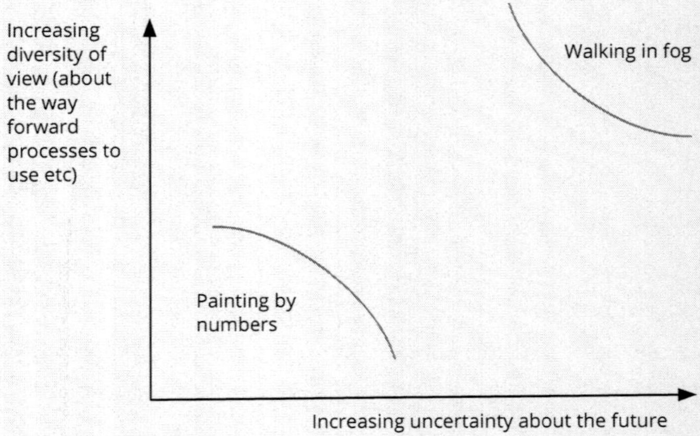

Figure 7 **Exploring the project at hand**
Source Visible Dynamics

When you are working on a project in the top right, it's like Walking in Fog. When walking in fog the best approach is to set out to explore and understand the uncertainty. You make progress by explicitly exploring the terrain, aiming to put stakes in the ground as you gain clarity, and making informed decisions about where to look next to reduce the uncertainty further.

Working in this way, you move from the top right towards the middle of *Figure 7*, eventually developing enough experience of the terrain to make realistic risk assessments.

When you reach this point it's appropriate to adopt more traditional approaches to project planning and risk management. Approaches which are akin to Painting by Numbers. Essentially, there is sufficient outline of the way forward to make filling in the detail relatively straightforward.

Exploring complexity in this way enables you to value the contribution and experience of those with an orientation towards certainty whilst opening a space that makes it possible for them to tolerate discussion about uncertainty, and vice versa. It does this in several ways.

First, it allows a seamless shift in language from uncertainty to risk without making judgement about which is more appropriate (Figure 8). Second, by using metaphor, it provides a language to talk about individual preferences and to compare expectations about the journey ahead.

These expectations go beyond the rational discourse that characterises most project – related conversations, (strategies, objectives, activities, risks etc).

Earlier we said the human brain is wired for survival, it trusts its own experience above all else. We are constantly comparing the current moment to past experience and making unconscious assumptions about what will happen next. These assumptions drive our thoughts, emotions and behaviours.

They inform what I call our 'inner, personal expectations'. Expectations which are determined by how we imagine, and sometimes fear, the project will or might unfold. In contrast to business-related expectations (*Figure 9*), inner expectations rarely figure explicitly in project-related conversations. Yet, they have an impact. They contribute to the dynamics and the emotional content and they determine the tone.

- Risks are associated with clarity and predictability – they can be quantified through a rational assessment of how likely, based on past experience, an event is to occur. These assessments are the basis of risk management approaches
- Uncertainties are assumptions associated with ambiguity and novelty – they are difficult to articulate and define, but this shouldn't prevent you treating them seriously and exploring them carefully. After all, uncertainties that come to pass have a real, and sometimes catastrophic, impact on delivery and outcomes

Figure 8 **Risk and Uncertainty**[13]

Inner, personal expectations include thoughts and feelings which are hard to admit in public, and sometimes hard to admit to ourselves. They appear in the stories we tell ourselves about what will happen and what has happened. Stories which vary depending on who we are talking to and how safe we feel.

It's easy to dismiss inner, personal expectations as irrational – until we view them through a neuroscience lens. Then it becomes clear that we need to take them seriously.

PROJECT EXPECTATIONS

BUSINESS RELATED EXPECTATIONS

all the things we usually talk about including

- Business objectives
- Strategies
- Systems & processes
- Plans
- Risks
- Finance

PERSONAL, INNER EXPECTATIONS

Thoughts and feelings we don't speak about (and often don't admit to ourselves) including

- What we imagine of fear the project will be like
- Based on
  - our past experiences
  - stories we've heard from others
  - what's happening right now (in the room, and elsewhere in our lives)

Figure 9 **Project expectations**
Source Visible Dynamics

Exploring Preferences

Each of us has a natural preference for different spaces on *Figure 7*.

I have worked with people who love being in the top right corner and Walking in Fog. They are energised by the constant uncertainty and relationship building required to deliver. Put them into stable situations requiring Painting by Numbers and they are like caged birds.

I have worked with others who are most comfortable Painting by Numbers and experience working with uncertainty as stressful.

When you understand how the human brain works it is clear that no place on the plot is better than another. What's important is the ability to recognise preferences (your own and others') and the implications.

With *thinking* brains online, we can use this framework and its metaphors to implicitly connect with the inner, unspoken expectations of project delivery.

Take time to tune in to stakeholders explaining why they believe this part of the project is foggy, and you'll be able to detect how comfortable they are with this amount of uncertainty. If you really pay attention, you can't help but empathise. The human brain works in such a way that you'll unconsciously pick up on their feelings and assumptions. These will give you clues about what explore.

Working with your stakeholders you'll be able to drill down and uncover, possibly for the first time, the aspects of the project that each of you find particularly ambiguous and worrisome. Together you'll be able to develop focussed strategies for dealing with uncertainty.

Part 3 – Key Lessons

- Organisations and projects are infinitely more relationally complex than is currently acknowledged
- To deal with this complexity it is crucial that leaders and project professionals
    - have an understanding of how the brain works
    - recognise that self protection is natural
    - learn to 'keep their *thinking* brain online'
    - know how to create psychologically safe environments
    - are comfortable exploring uncertainty
    - develop the skill to explore personal, inner expectations as easily as business related expectations
- Excess stress can trigger a Project Stress Cycle and disrupt delivery
- When starting a new project or taking over an existing one
    - recognise the nature of the journey you are embarking on
    - be explicit and label the project appropriately (Walking in Fog, Painting by Numbers)
    - remember that risk and uncertainty are 'in the eye of the beholder'

- When Walking in Fog
    - tell your stakeholders – literally!
    - talk about uncertainties, what you don't know and what you need to discover
    - ask them what they are uncertain about and where they feel most exposed
    - explain it may be uncomfortable, especially if they or others expect to be Painting by Numbers
    - be confident that done right, the fog will clear, you'll be able to turn uncertainties into risks – even though the fog will be patchy for a while
    - be ready to change approach and start Painting by Numbers where the fog has cleared sufficiently

References

1 The Evolution of Project Auditing, 2015 Global Benchmark Study. Retrieved from: https://www.iia.nl/SiteFiles/Publicaties/Project_Auditing_Global_Study_REPORT_MIC_IIA_NL_2015.pdf

2 Williams, T., Klakegg, O. J., Walker, D. H. T., Andersen, B., & Magnussen, O. M. (2012). Identifying and acting on early warning signs in complex projects. Project Management Journal, 43(2), 37–53. doi: http://dx.doi.org/10.1002/pmj.21259

3 McLean,P. (1990) The Triune Brain in Evolution, Plenium Press, New York

4 Siegel,D. *Hand Model of the Brain*. online video clip. Youtube 23 July 2015, Retrieved from https://www.youtube.com/watch?v=qFTljLo1bK8 , 7 March 2018

5 Rock, D (2009) *Managing with the Brain in Mind* Strategy +Business, Autumn 2009, Issue 56 Retrieved from: https://www.strategy-business.com/article/09306?gko=5df7f

6 Cecil in Kingsley, J. Brown,P, & Paterson, S. (2015) The Fear free Organisation: Vital Insights from Neuroscience to Transform Your Business Culture, London: Kogan Page) p 97

7 Duhigg, C. (25 Feb 2016) *What Google Learned From Its Quest to Build the Perfect Team Retrieved from:* The New York Times, https://www.nytimes.com/2016/02/28/magazine/what-google-learned-from-its-quest-to-build-the-perfect-team.html

8 Williams M, quoted on http://www.mindfulnet.org/index.htm

9 Kurtz,C.F. and Snowden, D.J (2003) *The new dynamics of strategy: Sense-making in a complex and complicated world* Retrieved from http://alumni.media.mit.edu/~brooks/storybiz/kurtz.pdf

10 Phillips, M. (June 2014), *Defining Complexity for Practitioners* PM World Journal, Vol. III, Issue VI www.pmworldjournal.net Retrieved from http://pmworldjournal.net/article/defining-complexity-practitioners/

11 Obeng,E. (1994) *All Change! The Project Leader's Secret Handbook*, London: Pitman p99

12 Stacey RD. (2002) *Strategic management and organisational dynamics: the challenge of complexity*. 3rd ed. Harlow: Prentice Hall

13 Kutsch E, Hall M &Turner N, (2015) Project Resilience: The Art of Noticing, Interpreting, Preparing, Containing and Recovering, London: Gower pp7-10

About the Author

Carole Osterweil is a consultant, speaker and educator. She is founder of Visible Dynamics, a consultancy set up to bring expertise from the emerging discipline of neuroscience to the world of complex change and transformation.

Her ambition is to empower those she works with to understand how the human brain works so they can use this knowledge to enable, rather than disable, individual and organisational change.

She's an executive coach at Ashridge Executive Education, part of Hult International Business School. In 2016 she became one of a handful of Project Academy coaches working with Cranfield University and PA Consulting to increase the UK Government's transformation and project leadership capability.

You can find her online at **www.visibledynamics.co.uk**

Let's Connect

I am constantly developing new resources to support my coaching and consulting clients and colleagues, so keep in touch via **www.visibledynamics.co.uk** for the latest information, join the **Project Mind** group on LinkedIn and tweet me **@CaroleOsterweil**

Feel free to share your experience of engaging with the book and let me know how the ideas here are supporting your work with complex projects, change and transformation.

48876165R00027

Printed in Poland
by Amazon Fulfillment
Poland Sp. z o.o., Wrocław